MORE
SLOW COOKING

 LAKELAND

Lakeland and Bauer Media Ltd hereby
exclude all liability to the extent permitted
by law for any errors or omission in
this book and for any loss, damage or
expense (whether direct or indirect)
suffered by a third party relying on any
information contained in this book.

This book was created in 2012 for
Lakeland by AWW Books,
an imprint of Octopus Publishing Group
Ltd, based on materials licensed to it
by Bauer Media Books, Sydney.

54 Park St, Sydney
GPO Box 4088, Sydney, NSW 2001
phone (02) 9282 8618; fax (02) 9267 9438
www.awwcookbooks.com.au

BAUER
MEDIA GROUP

OCTOPUS PUBLISHING GROUP
Design – Chris Bell
Food Director – Pamela Clark

Published for Lakeland in the United
Kingdom by Octopus Publishing
Group Limited

Endeavour House
189 Shaftesbury Avenue
London WC2H 8JY
United Kingdom
phone + 44 (0) 207 632 5400;
fax + 44 (0) 207 632 5405
aww@octopusbooks.co.uk;
www.octopusbooks.co.uk
www.australian-womens-weekly.com

Printed and bound in China

A catalogue record for this book is
available from the British Library.

ISBN 978-1-907428-76-0

The Department of Health advises that
eggs should not be consumed raw.
This book contains some dishes made
with raw or lightly cooked eggs. It is
prudent for vulnerable people such as
pregnant and nursing mothers, invalids,
the elderly, babies and young children to
avoid uncooked or lightly cooked dishes
made with eggs. Once prepared, these
dishes should be kept refrigerated and
used promptly.

This book also includes dishes made with
nuts and nut derivatives. It is advisable
for those with known allergic reactions to
nuts and nut derivatives and those who
may be potentially vulnerable to these
allergies, such as pregnant and nursing
mothers, invalids, the elderly, babies and
children to avoid dishes made with nuts
and nut oils. It is also prudent to check the
labels of pre-prepared ingredients for the
possible inclusion of nut derivatives.

Some of the recipes in this book have
appeared in other publications.

MORE SLOW COOKING

From Greek Lamb Stifado and Andalusian Pork to Chicken Tikka Masala and Spinach & Ricotta Lasagne, this collection of over 60 tempting recipes from around the world demonstrates just how versatile your slow cooker can be.

One of an exciting new series of cookbooks from Lakeland, *More Slow Cooking* is packed with delicious colour photos and expert hints, tips and techniques for beginners and experienced cooks alike.

With every recipe triple-tested® for perfect results, these excellent cookbooks are sure to be some of the best-loved on your kitchen bookshelf. To discover the rest of the range, together with our unrivalled selection of creative kitchenware, visit one of our friendly Lakeland stores or shop online at www.lakeland.co.uk.

CONTENTS

BREAKFAST AND LUNCHEON DISHES.   9

... to 3 pints water, 1/4
... and drop oatmeal
... 1/2 to 3/4 hour, stirring
... serve with cream or milk
... treacle, or butter.

SCRAMBLED EGGS.

Ingredients.—4 eggs, 1 teaspoon chopped parsley, 2 oz.
butter, salt and pepper to taste, and about 1/2 cup of milk.
Method.—Beat eggs well, add to them pepper, salt, parsley
and milk, and stir well; melt butter in a saucepan, stir eggs
it, and beat well over fire until it thickens; do not
harden. Serve on hot slices of buttered toast.

ALL ABOUT
SLOW COOKING

Slow cookers are available in a range of shapes and sizes and come with a host of features. We tested the recipes in this cookbook using a 4.5-litre slow cooker. If you have a smaller or larger cooker you will have to decrease or increase the quantity of ingredients and almost certainly adjust the liquid content too, to suit the size of cooker you have.

The first step when using your slow cooker is to read the manufacturer's instructions carefully as each slow cooker will have different features. Some cookers heat from the base and the sides, while others heat from the base only. Some have timers that cut off when the cooking time has expired and others have timers that allow you to keep food warm by reducing the temperature until you are ready to serve.

SLOW COOKER SETTINGS

The longer meat takes to cook, the more tender it will be and the more intense the flavour will be. If you have the time, set your cooker to a low setting. If you are short of time, setting the cooker on high will halve the cooking time. No matter which setting you use, the food will reach its simmering point.

HOW MUCH LIQUID DO I NEED?

Casseroles, stews and curries As a general rule, the slow cooker should be at least half full when cooking these dishes. Put then vegetables into the cooker, then the meat on top and then add the liquid.

Soups These are the simplest of all recipes to prepare in a slow cooker; just make sure that the cooker is at least half full.

Roasts Whole pieces of meat or poultry need minimal liquid content, especially if they are cooked on a bed of vegetables. Sometimes a little liquid is added as the basis of a sauce or gravy.

LIFTING THE LID

Tempting though it is to check on the progress of your meal, lifting the lid of the cooker constantly causes heat to escape and can set your cooking time back by up to half an hour.

The condensation that appears on the lid is the evaporation of moisture from the meat, sauce and vegetables. As the liquid evaporates it hits the lid and slowly bastes meat as it is cooking, ensuring that it is perfectly tender.

BROWNING MEAT

It is best to brown your meat before you add it to the slow cooker. Browning the meat first enhances the flavour and gives the meat a lovely, rich colour. Do this in a large, heated, oiled frying pan, adding the meat in batches and turning it so that is browns evenly. Make sure there is enough oil in the pan so that it caramelises, rather than scorches, and be sure to have the pan over a high heat. The pan should be large enough to make sure that the meat browns, rather than stews, which is what will happen if the pieces of meat are too close together.

If you are pushed for time, brown the meat the night before, place in a sealable container, along with the juices, and refrigerate overnight.

THICKENING THE SAUCE

Coating the meat in flour before browning will result in a sauce that is thick enough to make a light gravy. If the recipe does not suggest coating the meat, then you can thicken the sauce with flour or cornflour at the end of the cooking time.

Blending the cornflour or flour with butter or cold water or with some of the cooled juices from the cooker will help it to combine with the cooking juices when it is stirred into the slow cooker towards the end of the cooking time. Put the lid back on and leave the sauce to thicken while the slow cooker is on the highest setting; this will take 10–20 minutes.

If you don't want to use flour, another thickening tip is to blend some of the vegetables in the dish until smooth and then stir them into the cooking juices.

ABOUT FATS

Cooking meat over a long period can produce a lot of fat, which you will need to remove. The best way to do this is to refrigerate the cooked dish; the fat will set on top and can be simply lifted and discarded before reheating the dish. If you don't have time to do this, then one of the easiest ways to remove fat is to soak it up using sheets of absorbent kitchen towel.

USING DRIED BEANS

Some dried beans need to be cooked before being added to the slow cooker to prevent food poisoning. All kidney-shaped beans, of any colour or size, must be washed, drained and boiled in fresh water until they are tender. Then, like canned beans, they can be added to the rest of the ingredients in the cooker. Soya beans and chickpeas are fine to use raw. There is no need to soak them, just rinse them well first before adding to the slow cooker.

ADAPTING YOUR FAVOURITE RECIPES

Most of your favourite recipes for soups, curries, stews and casseroles are suitable for cooking in a slow cooker. You may need to adjust the liquid content to accommodate the long cooking time but, once you get to know your cooker, the possibilities are endless. For best results use recipes that you would normally cook slowly, well covered, in an oven set to a low temperature.

SLOW COOKER SAFETY

- Always read the manufacturer's instructions for your slow cooker before you begin cooking.
- Make sure the slow cooker is sitting securely on a flat surface away from water, any heat sources and out of reach of children or pets.
- The cord should be well away from water or heat sources and positioned so that there is no danger of it getting caught up on anything.
- The metal parts of the slow cooker get very hot so make sure no one touches them when the cooker is being used.
- Never submerge the base of the slow cooker in water.

SOUPS

CHICKEN, PORCINI & BARLEY SOUP

20g dried porcini mushrooms
250ml boiling water
2 chicken leg portions (700g)
1 medium brown onion (150g),
  chopped finely
2 cloves garlic, crushed
1 litre chicken stock
100g pearl barley
1 sprig fresh rosemary
1 sprig fresh thyme
1 medium parsnip (250g),
  chopped finely
1 small sweet potato (250g),
  chopped finely
2 stalks celery (300g), trimmed,
  chopped finely
250g chestnut mushrooms,
  quartered
6 tablespoons finely chopped
  fresh flat-leaf parsley

1 Place porcini in small heatproof bowl, cover with the water; stand about 15 minutes or until softened. Drain, reserve porcini and soaking liquid.
2 Meanwhile, discard as much skin as possible from chicken. Place chicken, onion, garlic, stock, barley, rosemary, thyme, parsnip, sweet potato, celery, chestnut mushrooms, porcini and strained soaking liquid into 4.5-litre slow cooker. Cook, covered, on low, 6 hours.
3 Remove chicken from cooker. When cool enough to handle, remove meat from bone; shred coarsely. Discard bones. Return meat to cooker; season to taste. Serve sprinkled with parsley.

prep + cook time 6 hours 30 minutes + standing time
serves 4
nutritional count per serving
9.4g total fat (3g saturated fat); 1488kJ (356 cal); 38.9g carbohydrate; 29.2g protein; 8.4g fibre
suitable to freeze at the end of step 3; sprinkle with parsley after reheating.

SHREDDED LAMB & PUMPKIN SOUP

100g dried brown lentils
3 french-trimmed lamb shanks
   (750g)
2 tablespoons moroccan
   seasoning
500g pumpkin, chopped coarsely
1 litre chicken stock
400g canned chopped tomatoes
400g canned chickpeas, rinsed,
   drained
6 tablespoons finely chopped
   fresh flat-leaf parsley

1 Rinse lentils under cold water until water runs clear; drain.
2 Combine lamb shanks, seasoning, pumpkin, stock, undrained tomatoes, chickpeas and lentils in 4.5-litre slow cooker. Cook, covered, on low, 6 hours.
3 Remove lamb from cooker. When cool enough to handle, remove meat from bones; shred coarsely. Discard bones. Return meat to cooker; season to taste. Serve sprinkled with parsley.

prep + cook time 6 hours 30 minutes
serves 4
nutritional count per serving 13g total fat (5.4g saturated fat); 1797kJ (430 cal); 34.7g carbohydrate; 39.7g protein; 10.3g fibre
suitable to freeze at the end of step 3; sprinkle with parsley after reheating.
serving suggestion Serve with a dollop of thick yogurt and crusty bread.

SPICY LENTIL SOUP

100g dried red lentils
1 litre chicken stock
400g canned chopped tomatoes
2 dried bay leaves
3 cloves garlic, crushed
100g mild indian curry paste
2 small carrots (240g), chopped
coarsely
1 stalk celery (150g), trimmed,
sliced thinly
2 medium potatoes (400g),
chopped coarsely
140g greek-style yogurt
6 tablespoons finely chopped
fresh coriander

1 Rinse lentils under cold water until water runs clear; drain.
2 Combine lentils, stock, undrained tomatoes, bay leaves, garlic, paste, carrot, celery and potato in 4.5-litre slow cooker. Cook, covered, on low, 6 hours. Season to taste.
3 Serve soup topped with yogurt and coriander.

prep + cook time 6 hours 30 minutes
serves 4
nutritional count per serving
12.5g total fat (3.4g saturated fat); 1421kJ (340 cal); 36.2g carbohydrate; 15.8g protein; 10.9g fibre
suitable to freeze at the end of step 2.

MULLIGATAWNY SOUP WITH CHICKEN

1 tablespoon vegetable oil
800g boneless chicken thighs,
    chopped coarsely
20g ghee
1 large brown onion (200g),
    chopped coarsely
2 stalks celery (300g), trimmed,
    chopped coarsely
2 medium carrots (240g),
    chopped coarsely
3 cloves garlic, chopped finely
75g madras curry paste
2 medium potatoes (400g),
    chopped coarsely
1 medium sweet potato (400g),
    chopped coarsely
100g dried red lentils, rinsed,
    drained
1.5 litres chicken stock
500ml coconut milk
3 tablespoons coarsely chopped
    fresh coriander

1 Heat oil in large frying pan;
cook chicken, in batches, until
browned. Transfer to 4.5-litre
slow cooker.
2 Heat ghee in same pan; cook
onion, celery and carrot, stirring,
until onion softens. Add garlic and
curry paste; cook, stirring, until
fragrant. Transfer to cooker with
potato, sweet potato, lentils, stock
and coconut milk. Cook, covered,
on low, 6 hours.
3 Stir in coriander and season
to taste.

prep + cook time 6 hours
30 minutes
serves 8
nutritional count per serving
28.5g total fat (16g saturated
fat); 1981kJ (474 cal); 24.7g
carbohydrate; 27.9g protein;
6.8g fibre
suitable to freeze at the end
of step 2. Stir in coriander after
reheating.
serving suggestion Serve with
roti bread, yogurt and lemon
wedges.
tip Beef or lamb could be used in
this recipe, instead of the chicken.

CAULIFLOWER SOUP

40g butter
2 large brown onions (400g),
    chopped coarsely
3 cloves garlic, crushed
1 litre vegetable stock
1.2kg cauliflower, cut into florets
2 medium potatoes (400g),
    chopped coarsely
500ml water
300ml single cream
2 tablespoons finely chopped
    fresh flat-leaf parsley

1 Heat butter in large frying pan; cook onion, stirring, until softened. Add garlic; cook, stirring, until fragrant. Add stock; bring to the boil.
2 Transfer onion mixture to 4.5-litre slow cooker with cauliflower, potato and the water. Cook, covered, on low, 6½ hours.
3 Blend or process soup, in batches, until smooth. Return to cooker; stir in cream. Cook, covered, on high, about 30 minutes or until soup is hot. Season to taste. Sprinkle with parsley.

prep + cook time 7 hours 25 minutes
serves 8
nutritional count per serving 19.3g total fat (12.3g saturated fat); 1105kJ (264 cal); 114.9g carbohydrate; 6g protein; 4.1g fibre
suitable to freeze at the end of step 3. Sprinkle with parsley after reheating.
tip You will need about 2 small cauliflowers for this recipe.

MEAT

VEAL STROGANOFF

1.5kg veal shoulder
35g plain flour
1 tablespoon sweet paprika
2 medium brown onions (300g),
    chopped coarsely
3 cloves garlic, crushed
400g tiny button mushrooms
375ml beef stock
2 tablespoons tomato paste
120g soured cream
3 tablespoons coarsely chopped
    fresh flat-leaf parsley

1 Cut veal into 2.5cm pieces. Toss veal in combined flour and paprika to coat, shake off excess; place in 4.5-litre slow cooker. Sprinkle veal evenly with excess flour mixture.
2 Add onion, garlic and mushrooms to cooker; pour over combined stock and paste. Cook, covered, on low, 6 hours.
3 Stir in soured cream; season to taste. Serve sprinkled with parsley.

prep + cook time 6 hours 20 minutes
serves 6
nutritional count per serving 14.4g total fat (7g saturated fat); 1743kJ (416 cal); 10.2g carbohydrate; 59.5g protein; 3.2g fibre
suitable to freeze at the end of step 2. Add sour cream when reheating and sprinkle with parsley after reheating.
serving suggestion Serve with buttered fettuccine, mashed potato or steamed rice.

MEATBALLS IN TOMATO SAUCE

2 slices white bread (90g), crusts removed
125ml milk
1kg minced beef
1 large brown onion (200g), chopped finely
1 medium carrot (120g), grated finely
3 cloves garlic, crushed
1 egg
2 tablespoons tomato paste
½ teaspoon dried oregano
2 tablespoons finely chopped fresh basil
1 tablespoon olive oil
1 medium brown onion (150g), chopped finely, extra
2 cloves garlic, crushed, extra
400g canned chopped tomatoes
400g canned cherry tomatoes
2 tablespoons tomato paste, extra
250ml beef stock
3 tablespoons fresh basil leaves

1 Combine bread and milk in large bowl; stand 10 minutes. Add beef, onion, carrot, garlic, egg, paste, oregano and chopped basil, season; mix well. Shape level tablespoons of mixture into balls. Transfer to 4.5-litre slow cooker.
2 Heat oil in large frying pan; cook extra onion and garlic, stirring, until onion softens. Stir in undrained tomatoes, extra paste and stock; transfer to cooker. Cook, covered, on low, 6 hours. Season to taste.
3 Serve sprinkled with basil leaves.

prep + cook time 6 hours 35 minutes
serves 6
nutritional count per serving 18.1g total fat (7.5g saturated fat); 1689kJ (404 cal); 18.4g carbohydrate; 39.7g protein; 4.4g fibre
suitable to freeze at the end of step 2. Sprinkle with basil after reheating.
serving suggestion Serve meatballs with spaghetti or mashed potato, sprinkle with parmesan cheese.

SHREDDED BEEF TACOS

1kg piece braising steak
¼ teaspoon chilli powder
1 teaspoon each ground cumin, coriander and smoked paprika
250ml beef stock
2 tablespoons tomato paste
1 fresh long red chilli, sliced thinly
2 cloves garlic, crushed
6 large flour tortillas, warmed

1 Rub beef with combined spices; place in 4.5-litre slow cooker. Pour over combined stock, paste, chilli and garlic. Cook, covered, on low, 6 hours.
2 Remove beef from cooker. When cool enough to handle, shred meat coarsely using two forks. Discard half the liquid from slow cooker. Return meat to cooker; season to taste.
3 Serve shredded beef in tortillas.

prep + cook time 6 hours 20 minutes
makes 6
nutritional count per serving
8.2g total fat (2.5g saturated fat); 1354kJ (324 cal); 18.9g carbohydrate; 42.4g protein; 1.6g fibre
suitable to freeze at the end of step 2.
serving suggestion Serve with guacamole, tomato salsa, grated cheese, soured cream, shredded lettuce and fresh coriander leaves.

BRAISED BEEF WITH
RED WINE & MUSHROOM SAUCE

2 tablespoons vegetable oil
1.3kg piece beef blade steak
6 shallots (150g), chopped finely
1 stalk celery (150g), trimmed, chopped finely
1 medium carrot (120g), chopped finely
2 cloves garlic, crushed
2 sprigs fresh thyme
375ml dry red wine
250ml beef stock
2 tablespoons plain flour
2 tablespoons water
400g button mushrooms, halved
80ml single cream
2 teaspoons wholegrain mustard

1 Heat half the oil in large frying pan; cook beef, until browned all over. Transfer to 4.5-litre slow cooker.

2 Heat remaining oil in same pan; cook shallot, celery and carrot, stirring, until softened. Add garlic and thyme; cook, stirring, until fragrant. Add wine; bring to the boil. Boil, uncovered, until liquid is reduced by half. Transfer to cooker with stock; mix well.

3 Cook, covered, on low, 5 hours. Remove beef from cooker; cover with foil. Stand 15 minutes before slicing.

4 Meanwhile, strain liquid into large jug; discard solids. Blend flour with the water in small bowl until smooth. Return cooking liquid to cooker with flour mixture and mushrooms. Cook, uncovered, on high, about 30 minutes or until sauce thickens. Stir in cream and mustard; season to taste.

5 Serve sliced beef with sauce.

prep + cook time 6 hours
serves 6
nutritional count per serving
30.9g total fat (13.4g saturated fat); 2316kJ (554 cal); 5.8g carbohydrate; 51.6g protein; 2.9g fibre
not suitable to freeze
serving suggestion Serve with spinach mash and steamed green beans.
tip Blade steak is a shoulder cut. Beef silverside or rolled brisket are also suitable to use.

ITALIAN-STYLE CHILLI BEEF

1 tablespoon olive oil
750g lean minced beef
1 large brown onion (200g),
  chopped finely
3 cloves garlic, crushed
1 teaspoon dried chilli flakes
125ml dry red wine
125ml beef stock
2 medium red peppers (400g),
  chopped finely
500g bottled passata
2 small courgettes (240g),
  chopped finely
400g canned cannellini beans,
  rinsed, drained
6 tablespoons fresh small basil
  leaves

1 Heat oil in large frying pan;
cook beef and onion, stirring,
until beef is browned. Add garlic
and chilli; cook, stirring, about
1 minute or until fragrant. Add
wine; bring to the boil. Boil,
uncovered, about 1 minute or
until liquid is almost evaporated.
Transfer mince mixture to 4.5-litre
slow cooker.
2 Stir in the stock, peppers and
passata. Cook, covered, on low,
5 hours.
3 Stir in courgettes and beans.
Cook, covered, on low, 1 hour.
4 Coarsely chop half the basil.
Just before serving, stir in
chopped basil; season to taste.
Serve sprinkled with remaining
basil.

prep + cook time 6 hours
45 minutes
serves 6
nutritional count per serving
14.2g total fat (5.2g saturated
fat); 1329kJ (318 cal); 12.5g
carbohydrate; 29.7g protein;
4.9g fibre
suitable to freeze at the end of
step 3. Stir in chopped basil after
reheating.
serving suggestion Serve with
soft polenta or crusty bread.

OXTAIL STEW WITH RED WINE & PORT

2kg oxtail, cut into 5cm pieces
2 tablespoons plain flour
2 tablespoons vegetable oil
12 brown pickling onions (480g)
2 medium carrots (240g),
   chopped coarsely
1 stalk celery (150g), trimmed,
   sliced thickly
8 cloves garlic, peeled
375ml dry red wine
500ml port
500ml beef stock
4 sprigs fresh thyme
1 dried bay leaf

1 Trim excess fat from oxtail; toss oxtail in flour to coat, shake off excess. Heat half the oil in large frying pan; cook oxtail, in batches, until browned. Transfer to 4.5-litre slow cooker.
2 Meanwhile, peel onions, leaving root ends intact.
3 Heat remaining oil in same pan; cook onions, carrot, celery and garlic, stirring, about 5 minutes or until vegetables are browned lightly. Transfer to cooker. Add wine and port to pan; bring to the boil. Boil, uncovered, until reduced to 1 cup. Transfer to cooker with stock, thyme and bay leaf. Cook, covered, on low, 8 hours.
4 Discard thyme and bay leaf. Remove oxtail from cooker; cover to keep warm. Cook sauce, uncovered, on high, about 30 minutes or until thickened. Skim fat from surface. Season to taste. Return oxtail to sauce to heat through.

prep + cook time 9 hours 15 minutes
serves 8
nutritional count per serving 48.4g total fat (17.4g saturated fat); 2959kJ (708 cal); 14.5g carbohydrate; 30.9g protein; 2g fibre
suitable to freeze at the end of step 4.
serving suggestion Serve with potato, celeriac or parsnip purée.
tips Beef brisket, beef cheeks and braising steak are all suitable to use in this recipe. Oxtail may need to be ordered from the butcher. The stew is best made a day ahead and refrigerated to set the fat, which can then be removed from the surface of the stew.

BEEF POT AU FEU

9 brown pickling onions (360g)
1.5kg piece beef sirloin or blade
steak
2 teaspoons coarse ground black
pepper
150g piece smoked speck
400g baby carrots, trimmed
9 baby new potatoes (360g),
halved
3 stalks celery (450g), trimmed,
chopped coarsely
1 litre chicken stock
6 cloves garlic, peeled
1 sprig fresh rosemary
1 sprig fresh thyme
2 fresh bay leaves
1 tablespoon coarsely chopped
fresh flat-leaf parsley

1 Peel onions, leaving root ends
intact.
2 Rub beef all over with pepper.
Place in 4.5-litre slow cooker. Add
remaining ingredients. Cook,
covered, on low, 6 hours. Season
to taste.
3 Remove beef from cooker;
shred into large pieces. Discard
speck, herbs and bay leaves.
Skim fat from surface of broth.
Serve meat with vegetables and
broth. Sprinkle with parsley before
serving.

prep + cook time 6 hours
30 minutes
serves 6
nutritional count per serving
16.4g total fat (6.8g saturated
fat); 2094kJ (501 cal); 16.4g
carbohydrate; 69g protein;
4.6g fibre

suitable to freeze at the end
of step 3. After freezing, scrape
the fat from the surface before
reheating. Sprinkle with parsley
after reheating.
tip Blade steak is a shoulder cut.
Beef silverside or rolled brisket are
also suitable to use.

GREEK LAMB STIFADO

1kg boneless lamb shoulder
2 tablespoons plain flour
800g brown pickling onions
4 cloves garlic, chopped finely
2 fresh bay leaves
1 sprig fresh rosemary
1 sprig rigani (greek dried
    oregano)
1 cinnamon stick
1 teaspoon ground cumin
2 whole cloves
2 tablespoons red wine vinegar
2 tablespoons tomato paste
125ml dry red wine
500ml chicken stock
100g feta cheese, crumbled

1 Cut lamb into 5cm pieces. Toss lamb in flour to coat, shake off excess; place in 4.5-litre slow cooker. Sprinkle lamb evenly with excess flour.
2 Peel onions, leaving root ends intact. Add onions, garlic, herbs and spices to cooker. Pour over combined vinegar, paste, wine and stock. Cook, covered, on low, 6 hours. Discard bay leaves, rosemary, rigani, cinnamon and cloves. Season to taste.
3 Serve sprinkled with cheese and extra rigani.

prep + cook time 6 hours 40 minutes
serves 4
nutritional count per serving
20.6g total fat (10.7g saturated fat); 2207kJ (528 cal); 18.2g carbohydrate; 59.8g protein; 3.8g fibre
suitable to freeze at the end of step 2.
serving suggestion Serve with mashed potato.
tips To peel pickling onions, place them in a heatproof bowl, cover with boiling water; stand 2 minutes, drain. The skins will slip off easily. You can use dried marjoram instead of rigani.

BALTI LAMB & RICE MEATBALLS

750g minced lamb
150g uncooked jasmine rice
70g stale breadcrumbs
1 egg
2 tablespoons finely chopped
fresh coriander
150g balti curry paste
625ml water
400g canned chopped tomatoes
2 medium brown onions (300g),
chopped finely
650g baby aubergines, halved
lengthways, chopped coarsely
6 tablespoons fresh coriander
leaves, extra

1 Combine lamb, rice, breadcrumbs, egg and coriander in large bowl, season; roll level tablespoons of mixture into balls. Place on tray, cover; refrigerate 20 minutes.
2 Combine paste and the water in large jug; pour into 4.5-litre slow cooker. Stir in undrained tomatoes and onion; add meatballs and aubergines. Cook, covered, on high, 4 hours. Season to taste.
3 Serve sprinkled with extra coriander.

prep + cook time 4 hours 30 minutes + refrigeration time
serves 6
nutritional count per serving 19g total fat (5.4g saturated fat); 1969kJ (471 cal); 37.5g carbohydrate; 33.7g protein; 7.3g fibre
suitable to freeze at the end of step 2.
tip Make sure the meatballs are completely submerged in the liquid during cooking.

LAMB BIRYANI

40g ghee
40g flaked almonds
2 large brown onions (400g),
  sliced thinly
1 tablespoon vegetable oil
1.2kg boneless lamb shoulder,
  chopped coarsely
20g ghee, extra
4 cloves garlic, crushed
5cm piece fresh ginger (25g),
  grated
2 fresh long green chillies, sliced
  thinly
2 teaspoons each ground cumin
  and coriander
3 teaspoons garam masala
200g greek-style yogurt
6 tablespoons coarsely chopped
  fresh coriander
3 tablespoons coarsely chopped
  fresh mint
1 litre water
pinch saffron threads
2 tablespoons hot milk
400g basmati rice
6 tablespoons fresh coriander
  leaves

1 Heat half the ghee in large frying pan; cook nuts, stirring, until browned lightly. Remove from pan. Heat remaining ghee in same pan; cook onion, stirring, about 10 minutes or until soft and browned lightly. Remove from pan.
2 Heat oil in same pan; cook lamb, in batches, until browned. Transfer to 4.5-litre slow cooker. Heat extra ghee in same pan; cook garlic, ginger, chilli and spices, stirring, until fragrant. Remove from heat; stir in yogurt, chopped herbs and half the onion mixture. Transfer to cooker with half the water. Cook, covered, on low, 8 hours. Season to taste.
3 Meanwhile, sprinkle saffron over hot milk in small bowl; stand 15 minutes. Wash rice under cold water until water runs clear; drain. Combine rice and the remaining water in medium saucepan, cover; bring to the boil. Reduce heat; simmer, covered, about 8 minutes or until rice is tender. Season to taste.

4 Spoon rice over lamb in cooker; drizzle with milk mixture. Top with remaining onion mixture and nuts; cook, covered, about 30 minutes or until heated through.
5 Serve sprinkled with coriander leaves.

prep + cook time 9 hours
serves 8
nutritional count per serving
24.2g total fat (11.2g saturated fat); 2307kJ (552 cal); 45.2g carbohydrate; 36.8g protein; 2.1g fibre
not suitable to freeze
serving suggestion Serve with raita and lime wedges.

LAMB CHOPS WITH ANCHOVIES, CHILLI & CAVOLO NERO

1.5kg lamb shoulder chops
2 tablespoons plain flour
80ml olive oil
4 cloves garlic, sliced thinly
8 drained anchovy fillets,
    chopped finely
2 fresh long red chillies, sliced
    thinly
125ml dry white wine
375ml chicken stock
100g cavolo nero, chopped
    coarsely
6 tablespoons coarsely chopped
    fresh flat-leaf parsley

1 Trim excess fat from lamb. Toss lamb in flour to coat, shake off excess. Reserve excess flour. Heat 1 tablespoon of the oil in large frying pan; cook lamb, in batches, until browned. Transfer to 4.5-litre slow cooker. Sprinkle reserved excess flour over lamb.
2 Wipe out pan with absorbent paper. Heat remaining oil in same pan; cook garlic, anchovy and chilli, stirring, until anchovies are soft. Add wine; bring to the boil. Boil, uncovered, until liquid is almost evaporated. Add stock; bring to the boil.
3 Transfer stock mixture to cooker. Cook, covered, on low, 6 hours.
4 Add cavolo nero; cook, covered, on low, about 30 minutes or until cavolo nero wilts. Season to taste. Stir in parsley.

prep + cook time 7 hours
serves 6
nutritional count per serving
20.1g total fat (5.4g saturated fat); 1387kJ (332 cal); 4.3g carbohydrate; 29.5g protein; 1.2g fibre
suitable to freeze at the end of step 3.
serving suggestion Serve with creamy polenta, mashed potato or risotto.
tip You can use swiss chard, kale or savoy cabbage instead of cavolo nero.

LAMB STEW WITH ARTICHOKES & PEAS

1.5kg lamb shoulder chops
2 tablespoons plain flour
2 tablespoons olive oil
12 fresh sage leaves
1 large brown onion (200g),
  chopped coarsely
2 stalks celery (300g), trimmed,
  chopped coarsely
1 large carrot (180g), chopped
  coarsely
4 cloves garlic, chopped finely
125ml dry white wine
375ml chicken stock
1 tablespoon coarsely chopped
  fresh sage
60g frozen peas
360g small fresh artichokes,
  trimmed, halved, centre chokes
  removed

1 Trim excess fat from lamb. Toss lamb in flour to coat, shake off excess. Reserve excess flour. Heat half the oil in large frying pan, cook sage leaves until browned lightly and crisp; drain on absorbent paper.
2 Cook lamb in same pan, in batches, until browned. Transfer to 4.5-litre slow cooker. Sprinkle reserved excess flour over lamb.
3 Heat remaining oil in same pan; cook onion, celery and carrot, stirring, until softened. Add garlic; cook, stirring, until fragrant. Add wine; bring to the boil. Boil, uncovered, until liquid is almost evaporated. Stir onion mixture, stock and extra sage into cooker. Cook, covered, on low, 6 hours.
4 Add peas and artichokes to cooker; cook, covered, 30 minutes. Season to taste. Serve sprinkled with crisp sage leaves.

prep + cook time 7 hours
serves 6
nutritional count per serving
14g total fat (4.5g saturated fat); 1271kJ (304 cal); 8.9g carbohydrate; 30.1g protein; 4g fibre
suitable to freeze at the end of step 3.
tip Lamb loin and chump chops are also suitable for this recipe.

FRENCH ONION LAMB CHOPS

2kg lamb shoulder chops
2 tablespoons plain flour
2 tablespoons olive oil
80g packaged french onion soup
    mix
2 medium leeks (700g), sliced
    thinly
3 stalks celery (450g), trimmed,
    chopped coarsely
500m chicken stock
3 tablespoons coarsely chopped
    fresh flat-leaf parsley

1 Trim excess fat from lamb. Toss lamb in flour to coat, shake off excess. Heat oil in large frying pan; cook lamb, in batches, until browned.
2 Place 4 lamb chops into 4.5-litre slow cooker. Sprinkle one-third of the soup mix then one-third of the leek and celery over the chops. Repeat layering with remaining lamb, soup mix, leek and celery. Pour stock into cooker. Cook, covered, on low, 6 hours.
3 Remove lamb from cooker; cover to keep warm. Skim fat from surface of sauce; season to taste. Serve lamb and sauce sprinkled with parsley.

prep + cook time 6 hours 30 minutes
serves 12
nutritional count per serving 8.5g total fat (2.9g saturated fat); 765kJ (183 cal); 5.8g carbohydrate; 19.9g protein; 2.2g fibre
suitable to freeze at the end of step 3. Sprinkle over parsley after reheating.
serving suggestion Serve with mashed or roast potatoes, and steamed green beans.
tip Lamb loin and chump chops are also suitable for this recipe.

MEXICAN PULL-APART PORK

2 medium red peppers (400g),
  sliced thinly
2 medium brown onions (300g),
  sliced thinly
375g bottled chunky mild tomato
  salsa
280g barbecue sauce
4 cloves garlic, crushed
3 teaspoons ground cumin
2 teaspoons cayenne pepper
1 teaspoon dried oregano
1kg boneless pork shoulder
12 large flour tortillas

1 Combine peppers, onion, salsa, sauce, garlic, spices and oregano in 4.5-litre slow cooker; add pork, turn to coat in mixture. Cook, covered, on low, 8 hours.
2 Carefully remove pork from cooker; shred meat using two forks. Return pork to cooker; stir gently. Season to taste.
3 Divide pork between tortillas.

prep + cook time 8 hours 20 minutes
serves 6
nutritional count per serving
26.3g total fat (13.2g saturated fat); 2842kJ (680 cal); 66.5g carbohydrate; 42.5g protein; 5.4g fibre
suitable to freeze at the end of step 2.
serving suggestion Serve with soured cream, lime wedges and fresh coriander leaves.
tip You can quickly peel the peppers with a vegetable peeler if you don't like the skin peeling off when they are cooked.

BARBECUED AMERICAN-STYLE PORK RIBS

2kg pork rib rack
140g barbecue sauce
140g tomato ketchup
125ml cider vinegar
85g orange marmalade
3 cloves garlic, crushed
½ teaspoon chilli flakes

1 Cut pork into pieces to fit into cooker. Combine remaining ingredients in large shallow dish; add pork, turn to coat in marinade. Cover; refrigerate mixture overnight.

2 Transfer pork and marinade to 4.5-litre slow cooker; cook, covered, on high, 4 hours. Turn ribs twice during cooking time for even cooking.

3 Carefully remove ribs from cooker; cover to keep warm. Transfer sauce to large frying pan; bring to the boil. Reduce heat; simmer, uncovered, skimming fat from surface, for about 10 minutes or until sauce has reduced to about 430ml. Serve pork drizzled with sauce.

prep + cook time 4 hours 30 minutes + refrigeration time
serves 4
nutritional count per serving 10.6g total fat (3.8g saturated fat); 1860kJ (445 cal); 38.2g carbohydrate; 48.6g protein; 1.7g fibre
suitable to freeze at the end of step 3.
serving suggestion Serve with steamed rice and lime wedges.

ITALIAN PORK & PEPPER RAGÙ

2 tablespoons olive oil

1.6kg rindless boneless belly of pork, chopped coarsely

4 italian-style thin pork sausages (310g)

3 medium red peppers (600g), sliced thickly

2 medium brown onions (300g), sliced thinly

1.2kg canned white beans, rinsed, drained

6 cloves garlic, crushed

400g canned chopped tomatoes

310ml chicken stock

1 tablespoon tomato paste

1 teaspoon dried oregano

½ teaspoon chilli flakes

3 tablespoons fresh oregano leaves

1 Heat oil in large frying pan; cook pork, in batches, until browned. Transfer to 4.5-litre slow cooker.

2 Cook sausages in same pan until browned; transfer to cooker with pepper, onion, beans, garlic, undrained tomatoes, stock, paste, dried oregano and chilli. Cook, covered, on low, 8 hours.

3 Skim fat from surface. Season ragù to taste; serve sprinkled with fresh oregano.

prep + cook time 8 hours 30 minutes

serves 8

nutritional count per serving
24.8g total fat (8g saturated fat); 2006kJ (480 cal); 10.9g carbohydrate; 51.6g protein; 5g fibre

suitable to freeze at the end of step 2. Sprinkle with oregano after reheating.

tip Italian-style pork sausages are coarse pork sausages, usually flavoured with garlic and fennel seed or aniseed. You can use any spicy pork sausages instead.

CHICKEN

POACHED CHICKEN WITH SOY & SESAME

1.6kg whole chicken
5cm piece fresh ginger (25g),
   sliced thinly
4 cloves garlic, halved
2 star anise
2 cinnamon sticks
250ml light soy sauce
250ml chinese cooking wine
75g granulated sugar
1 litre water
80ml light soy sauce, extra
2 teaspoons sesame oil
2 cloves garlic, cut into
   matchsticks
2.5cm piece fresh ginger (15g),
   cut into matchsticks
2 fresh long red chillies, sliced
   thinly
80ml groundnut oil
4 spring onions, sliced thinly
6 tablespoons fresh coriander
   leaves

1 Trim excess fat from chicken. Place chicken in 4.5-litre slow cooker. Add sliced ginger, halved garlic, star anise, cinnamon, sauce, wine, sugar and the water to cooker. Cook, covered, on low, 6 hours. Remove chicken from cooker; discard poaching liquid.
2 Cut chicken into 12 pieces; place on heatproof platter. Drizzle extra sauce and sesame oil over chicken; sprinkle with garlic and ginger matchsticks and chilli.
3 Heat groundnut oil in small saucepan, over medium heat, until very hot; carefully drizzle over chicken. Top with onion and coriander.

prep + cook time 6 hours 20 minutes
serves 4
nutritional count per serving
52.9g total fat (13.7g saturated fat); 3361kJ (804 cal); 22.7g carbohydrate; 45.5g protein; 1.5g fibre
suitable to freeze at the end of step 1.
serving suggestion Serve with steamed noodles or rice.
tip Chinese cooking wine is also known as chinese rice wine or shao hsing wine; dry sherry can be used instead.

POULE-AU-POT

12 brown pickling onions (480g)
750g new potatoes, unpeeled
1.8kg whole chicken
3 medium carrots (660g),
    chopped coarsely
2 medium turnips (460g), halved
1 dried bay leaf
3 sprigs fresh thyme
1 teaspoon black peppercorns
1 litre water
2 teaspoons fresh thyme leaves,
    extra

1 Peel onions, leaving root ends intact. Wash and scrub potatoes well.
2 Place chicken in 4.5-litre slow cooker; place carrot, turnip and onion around chicken. Add bay leaf, thyme and peppercorns; top with potatoes. Pour the water into cooker. Cook, covered, on low, 8 hours.
3 Serve chicken and vegetables with a little of the broth; sprinkle with extra thyme.

prep + cook time 8 hours 20 minutes
serves 6
nutritional count per serving
31.7g total fat (9.6g saturated fat); 2747kJ (656 cal); 27.4g carbohydrate; 61g protein; 8.3g fibre
not suitable to freeze
serving suggestion Serve with dijon mustard and crusty bread.
tip Leftover broth can be used as chicken stock in soup or stews.

GREEN CHICKEN CURRY

1kg boneless chicken thighs, halved

2 cloves garlic, crushed

2.5cm piece fresh ginger (15g), grated

1 fresh long green chilli, chopped finely

2 tablespoons green curry paste

2 fresh kaffir lime leaves, torn

230g canned sliced bamboo shoots, rinsed, drained

400g canned baby corn, rinsed, drained, chopped coarsely

180ml chicken stock

410ml coconut milk

2 tablespoons cornflour

1 tablespoon water

1 tablespoon grated palm sugar

1 tablespoon lime juice

1 tablespoon fish sauce

1 large handful fresh thai basil leaves

4 tablespoons fresh coriander leaves

1 Combine chicken, garlic, ginger, chilli, paste, lime leaves, bamboo shoots, corn, stock and coconut milk in 4.5-litre slow cooker. Cook, covered, on low, 4 hours.

2 Blend cornflour with the water in small bowl until smooth. Stir cornflour mixture, sugar, juice, sauce and half the basil into cooker. Cook, uncovered, on high, about 20 minutes or until thickened slightly. Season to taste. Serve sprinkled with coriander and remaining basil.

prep + cook time 4 hours 45 minutes
serves 6
nutritional count per serving 29.2g total fat (16.4g saturated fat); 1981kJ (474 cal); 16.2g carbohydrate; 35.4g protein; 4.7g fibre
suitable to freeze at the end of step 1.
serving suggestion Serve with steamed jasmine rice and lime wedges.
tip You can use dried kaffir lime leaves if you can't get fresh and can use sweet or Greek basil instead of Thai basil.

CHICKEN, CELERIAC & BROAD BEAN CASSEROLE

1.5kg boneless chicken thighs
2 tablespoons plain flour
2 tablespoons vegetable oil
20g butter
1 large brown onion (200g),
    chopped coarsely
2 medium carrots (240g), sliced
    thickly
2 stalks celery (300g), trimmed,
    chopped coarsely
2 cloves garlic, chopped finely
500ml chicken stock
2 tablespoons dijon mustard
1 medium celeriac (750g),
    chopped coarsely
300g frozen broad beans
50g walnuts, roasted, chopped
    coarsely
3 tablespoons coarsely chopped
    pale celery leaves

1 Toss chicken in flour to coat, shake off excess. Reserve excess flour. Heat oil in large frying pan; cook chicken, in batches, until browned. Remove from pan. Wipe pan with absorbent paper.
2 Heat butter in same pan; cook onion, carrot and celery, stirring, until softened. Add garlic; cook, stirring, until fragrant. Stir in reserved excess flour, then stock and mustard; stir over high heat until mixture boils and thickens.
3 Place celeriac in 4.5-litre slow cooker. Top with chicken then onion mixture. Cook, covered, on high, 3 hours.
4 Meanwhile, place broad beans in medium heatproof bowl, cover with boiling water; stand 2 minutes, drain. Peel away grey skins.
5 Add broad beans to slow cooker; cook, covered, on high, 30 minutes. Season to taste.
6 Serve sprinkled with nuts and celery leaves.

prep + cook time 4 hours
serves 6
nutritional count per serving
33.4g total fat (8.6g saturated fat); 2504kJ (599 cal); 16.3g carbohydrate; 54.6g protein; 9.8g fibre
suitable to freeze at the end of step 3.
tip Roast the walnuts, in a preheated 180°C/160°C fan-assisted oven, for about 5 minutes or until browned lightly.

JERK-SPICED CHICKEN DRUMSTICKS

2 tablespoons olive oil

8 chicken drumsticks (1.2kg)

4 spring onions, chopped coarsely

5cm piece fresh ginger (20g), grated

1½ teaspoons ground allspice

½ teaspoon ground cinnamon

2 fresh long green chillies, chopped coarsely

1 teaspoon coarse ground black pepper

2 cloves garlic, crushed

3 teaspoons finely chopped fresh thyme

2 tablespoons light brown sugar

1 tablespoon cider vinegar

2 tablespoons orange juice

1 Heat half the oil in large frying pan; cook chicken, turning, until browned all over. Place chicken in 4.5-litre slow cooker.

2 Meanwhile, process onion, ginger, spices, chilli, pepper, garlic, thyme and remaining oil until finely chopped. Add sugar, vinegar and juice; process until smooth. Pour paste over chicken. Cook, covered, on low, 4 hours. Season to taste.

3 Serve chicken with sauce; sprinkle with extra thyme.

prep + cook time 4 hours 30 minutes

serves 4

nutritional count per serving 30.1g total fat (7.6g saturated fat); 1831kJ (438 cal); 8.2g carbohydrate; 33.9g protein; 0.9g fibre

suitable to freeze at the end of step 2.

serving suggestion Serve with steamed green beans, rice and lime wedges.

CHICKEN TIKKA MASALA

1kg boneless, skinless chicken
  thighs
800g canned chopped tomatoes
2 large brown onions (400g),
  sliced thinly
200g tikka masala paste
60ml single cream
1 large handful fresh coriander
  leaves

1 Combine chicken, undrained tomatoes, onion and paste in 4.5-litre slow cooker; cook, covered, on high, 4 hours. Season to taste.
2 Drizzle with cream, sprinkle with coriander.

prep + cook time 4 hours 15 minutes
serves 6
nutritional count per serving
22.3g total fat (5.9g saturated fat); 1467kJ (351 cal); 10.8g carbohydrate; 24.2g protein; 6g fibre
suitable to freeze at the end of step 1.
serving suggestion Serve with steamed rice, naan bread and raita.

SPICED CHICKEN WITH DATES & CHICKPEAS

8 boneless, skinless chicken thighs (1.6kg)

2 tablespoons plain flour

2 tablespoons olive oil

2 medium brown onions (300g), cut into thin wedges

4 cloves garlic, chopped finely

1 fresh long red chilli, sliced thinly

2 teaspoons each ground cumin and cinnamon

¼ teaspoon saffron threads

2 tablespoons honey

500ml chicken stock

400g canned chickpeas, rinsed, drained

3 small courgettes (270g), sliced thickly

6 fresh dates (120g), halved, pitted

2 tablespoons lemon juice

4 tablespoons fresh coriander leaves

1 Toss chicken in flour to coat, shake off excess. Heat half the oil in large frying pan; cook chicken, in batches, until browned. Remove from pan.

2 Heat remaining oil in same pan; cook onion, stirring, until onion softens. Add garlic, chilli and spices; cook, stirring, about 2 minutes or until fragrant. Stir in honey.

3 Place half the chicken in 4.5-litre slow cooker; top with half the spice mixture. Top with remaining chicken then remaining spice mixture. Pour stock over chicken. Cook, covered, on low, 5 hours.

4 Add chickpeas, courgettes and dates around the outside edge of cooker. Cook, covered, 1 hour. Stir in juice; season to taste. Serve sprinkled with coriander.

prep + cook time 6 hours 25 minutes
serves 4
nutritional count per serving 31.3g total fat (7.8g saturated fat); 2926kJ (700 cal); 42.1g carbohydrate; 60.8g protein; 7.4g fibre
suitable to freeze at the end of step 3.
serving suggestion Serve with couscous or flat bread.

CHICKEN & CHORIZO PAELLA

1 tablespoon olive oil
500g chicken breast fillets,
    chopped coarsely
1 cured chorizo sausage (170g),
    sliced thinly
1 medium brown onion (150g),
    chopped finely
1 medium red pepper (200g),
    chopped finely
2 cloves garlic, crushed
½ teaspoon saffron threads
2 teaspoons smoked paprika
250ml chicken stock
400g canned chopped tomatoes
500g packaged microwave white
    long-grain rice
90g frozen peas
75g pimento-stuffed green olives
6 tablespoons finely chopped
    fresh flat-leaf parsley

1 Heat oil in large frying pan;
cook chicken and chorizo, in
batches, until browned. Transfer to
4.5-litre slow cooker.
2 Add onion, pepper, garlic,
spices, stock and undrained
tomatoes. Cook, covered, on low,
4 hours.
3 Stir in rice and peas. Cook,
covered, on low, about 15 minutes
or until hot. Season to taste. Serve
sprinkled with olives and parsley.

prep + cook time 5 hours
serves 4
nutritional count per serving
21.6g total fat (6.2g saturated
fat); 2320kJ (555 cal); 43.8g
carbohydrate; 42.9g protein;
6.2g fibre
not suitable to freeze

CREAMY LEMON THYME CHICKEN

2 tablespoons olive oil

1kg boneless chicken thighs, halved

2 medium brown onions (300g), sliced thinly

1 medium fennel bulb (300g), sliced thinly

4 sprigs fresh lemon thyme

2 cloves garlic, crushed

125ml dry white wine

2 tablespoons wholegrain mustard

1 medium sweet potato (400g), chopped coarsely

250ml chicken stock

180ml single cream

1 Heat half the oil in large frying pan; cook chicken, in batches, until browned. Transfer to 4.5-litre slow cooker.

2 Heat remaining oil in same pan; cook onion, stirring, about 10 minutes or until caramelised. Transfer to cooker with remaining ingredients. Cook, covered, on low, 4 hours. Discard thyme; season to taste.

prep + cook time 4 hours 30 minutes

serves 4

nutritional count per serving 47g total fat (19.7g saturated fat); 3076kJ (736 cal); 20.5g carbohydrate; 51.8g protein; 4.9g fibre

not suitable to freeze

serving suggestion Serve with mashed potato, pasta or rice.

CHEAT'S CHICKEN JAMBALAYA

500g chicken breast fillets, chopped coarsely

1 cured chorizo sausage (170g), sliced thinly

400g canned chopped tomatoes

1 medium green pepper (200g), sliced thickly

1 medium red pepper (200g), sliced thickly

1 stalk celery (300g), trimmed, sliced thinly

250ml chicken stock

1 teaspoon dried oregano

1 tablespoon cajun seasoning

pinch cayenne pepper

2 dried bay leaves

500g cooked shelled prawns

500g packaged 90-second microwave white long-grain rice

1 Combine chicken, chorizo, undrained tomatoes, peppers, celery, stock, oregano, seasoning, pepper and bay leaves in 4.5-litre slow cooker. Cook, covered, on low, 4 hours.

2 Stir in prawns and rice. Cook, covered, on low, about 15 minutes or until hot. Season to taste.

prep + cook time 4 hours 40 minutes
serves 4
nutritional count per serving 16.9g total fat (5.7g saturated fat); 2562kJ (613 cal); 41.6g carbohydrate; 71.2g protein; 3.2g fibre
not suitable to freeze
tip Use fresh or frozen (thawed) prawns.

SWEET & SOUR CHICKEN

1 tablespoon vegetable oil

4 skinless chicken drumsticks (520g)

4 boneless, skinless chicken thighs (800g)

2 medium red onions (340g), cut into wedges

125ml japanese soy sauce

130g bottled passata

80ml pineapple juice

2 tablespoons light brown sugar

2 tablespoons white vinegar

1 fresh long red chilli, chopped finely

2 cloves garlic, crushed

1 large red pepper (350g), chopped coarsely

1 large green pepper (350g), chopped coarsely

225g canned pineapple pieces in juice

2 tablespoons cornflour

2 tablespoons water

2 spring onions, shredded finely

1 Heat oil in large frying pan; cook chicken, in batches, until browned. Transfer to 4.5-litre slow cooker. Add red onion, sauce, passata, juice, sugar, vinegar, chilli, garlic, peppers and undrained pineapple. Cook, covered, on low, 4 hours.

2 Blend cornflour with the water in small bowl until smooth. Add cornflour mixture to cooker. Cook, uncovered, on high, about 5 minutes or until thickened. Season to taste.

3 Serve sprinkled with spring onion.

prep + cook time 4 hours 30 minutes

serves 4

nutritional count per serving 16.1g total fat (4.6g saturated fat); 1986kJ (475 cal); 31.7g carbohydrate; 47.8g protein; 4.7g fibre

suitable to freeze at the end of step 2.

tips Use whatever cuts of chicken you like for this recipe – choose cuts on the bones for a moist result.

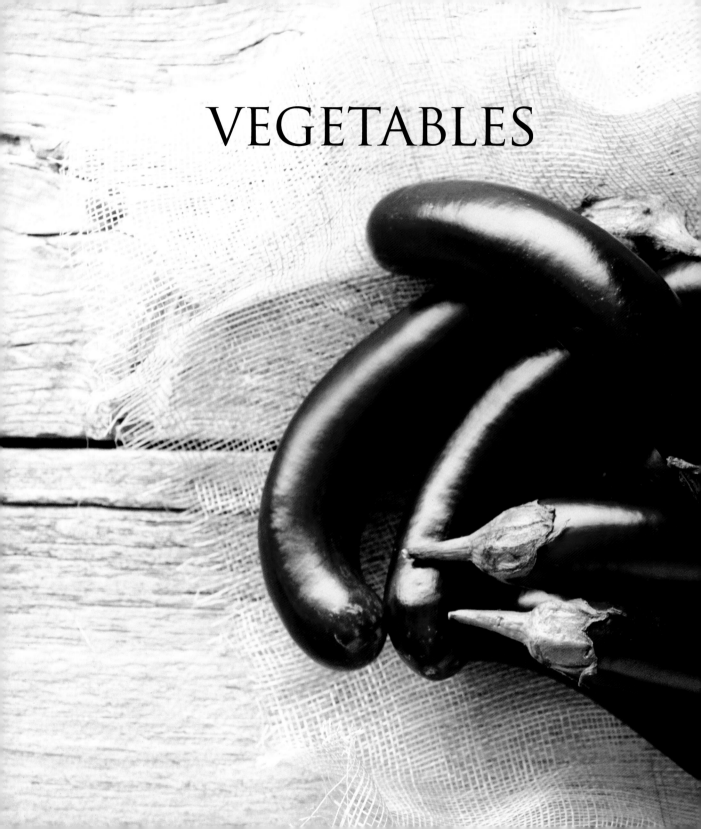

VEGETABLES

MOROCCAN-STYLE VEGETABLE STEW WITH HARISSA

1 medium red onion (170g), chopped coarsely

4 cloves garlic, quartered

2 teaspoons each ground cumin, coriander and sweet paprika

1 fresh long red chilli, chopped finely

6 tablespoons fresh flat-leaf parsley leaves and stalks, chopped coarsely

1 large handful fresh coriander leaves and stalks, chopped coarsely

500ml vegetable stock

4 baby aubergines (240g), chopped coarsely

4 small courgettes (360g), chopped coarsely

2 small parsnips (240g), chopped coarsely

2 medium carrots (240g), halved lengthways, then halved crossways

¼ medium butternut squash (500g), skin on, cut into 8 pieces

2 medium potatoes (400g), quartered

2 tablespoons honey

280g greek-style yogurt

1 tablespoon harissa

4 tablespoons fresh coriander leaves, extra

1 Blend or process onion, garlic and spices until smooth. Combine paste with chilli, herbs and stock in large jug.

2 Combine vegetables and stock mixture in 4.5-litre slow cooker. Cook, covered, on low, 6 hours. Stir in honey; season to taste.

3 Serve vegetables and sauce topped with yogurt, harissa and extra coriander.

prep + cook time 6 hours 45 minutes
serves 4
nutritional count per serving 12.2g total fat (5.3g saturated fat); 1659kJ (397 cal); 52.1g carbohydrate; 13.4g protein; 11.9g fibre
not suitable to freeze
serving suggestion Serve with buttered couscous.

MUSHROOM 'RISOTTO'

30g butter
1 large brown onion (200g),
  chopped finely
125ml dry white wine
1 litre vegetable stock
500ml water
10g dried porcini mushroom
  slices, torn
400g arborio rice
60g butter, extra
300g button mushrooms, sliced
  thinly
200g chestnut mushrooms, sliced
  thinly
2 cloves garlic, crushed
2 teaspoons finely chopped fresh
  thyme
80g finely grated parmesan
  cheese

1 Heat butter in large frying pan; cook onion, stirring, until softened. Add wine; bring to the boil. Boil, uncovered, until liquid is almost evaporated. Add stock, the water and porcini; bring to the boil.
2 Place rice in 4.5-litre slow cooker; stir in onion mixture. Cook, covered, on high, 1½ hours. Stir well.
3 Meanwhile, heat 20g of the extra butter in same pan; cook button mushrooms, stirring occasionally, until browned. Remove from pan. Heat another 20g butter in same pan; cook chestnut mushrooms, stirring occasionally, until browned. Add garlic and thyme; cook, stirring, until fragrant.
4 Stir button mushrooms and chestnut mushroom mixture into cooker. Cook, uncovered, on high, about 20 minutes or until rice is tender.
5 Stir in cheese and remaining butter; season to taste. Serve immediately, sprinkled with extra thyme and parmesan cheese.

prep + cook time 2 hours
40 minutes
serves 4
nutritional count per serving
26.6g total fat (16.6g saturated fat); 2947kJ (705 cal); 88.7g carbohydrate; 20g protein; 4.7g fibre
not suitable to freeze
tip This risotto has the texture of an oven-baked version rather than the creaminess of a traditional stirred risotto; it must be served immediately.

SPINACH & RICOTTA LASAGNE

500g frozen spinach, thawed
720g ricotta cheese
2 eggs
80g parmesan cheese, finely
    grated
cooking-oil spray
750g bottled passata
90g basil pesto
6 lasagne sheets
100g mozzarella cheese, coarsely
    grated

1 Squeeze excess moisture from spinach; place spinach in large bowl. Add ricotta, eggs and half the parmesan; mix well, season.
2 Spray the bowl of 4.5-litre slow cooker lightly with cooking oil. Combine passata and pesto in medium bowl, season; spread 125ml of the sauce mixture over base of cooker.
3 Place 2 lasagne sheets in cooker, breaking to fit. Spread one-third of the spinach mixture over pasta; top with one-third of the sauce, then 2 more lasagne sheets. Repeat layering, finishing with sauce. Sprinkle with mozzarella and remaining parmesan. Cook, covered, on low, 4 hours or until pasta is tender.

prep + cook time 4 hours 30 minutes
serves 6
nutritional count per serving
31.9g total fat (15.8g saturated fat); 2211kJ (529 cal); 25.1g carbohydrate; 32.7g protein; 8.3g fibre
suitable to freeze at the end of step 3.
serving suggestion Serve with a rocket salad, and some crusty bread.

OKRA CURRY

60ml groundnut oil
2 large brown onions (400g),
 sliced thinly
2 fresh long green chillies,
 quartered lengthways
4cm piece fresh ginger (20g),
 grated
5 cloves garlic, crushed
2 teaspoons ground coriander
1 teaspoon garam masala
½ teaspoon each ground turmeric
 and chilli powder
2 medium tomatoes (300g),
 chopped coarsely
1kg okra, trimmed
625ml coconut milk

1 Heat oil in large saucepan; cook onion, stirring, until soft and browned lightly. Add chilli, ginger and garlic; cook, stirring, until fragrant. Stir in spices; cook, stirring, 1 minute. Add tomato; cook, stirring, 2 minutes.
2 Transfer tomato mixture to 4.5-litre slow cooker with okra and coconut milk; season. Cook, covered, on high, 2½ hours.

prep + cook time 3 hours
serves 4
nutritional count per serving
46.8g total fat (30.9g saturated fat); 2395kJ (573 cal); 17.4g carbohydrate; 14g protein; 16.9g fibre
suitable to freeze at the end of step 2.
serving suggestion Serve with steamed rice and lime wedges.

CHANA MASALA

2 large brown onions (400g),
chopped coarsely
8 cloves garlic, quartered
6cm piece fresh ginger (60g),
grated
2 tablespoons tomato paste
125g ghee
2 teaspoons each ground
coriander and garam masala
1 teaspoon ground turmeric
½ teaspoon ground chilli
800g canned chickpeas, rinsed,
drained
375ml water
6 tablespoons fresh coriander
leaves

1 Blend onion, garlic, ginger and paste until smooth.
2 Heat ghee in large saucepan; cook onion mixture, stirring, 5 minutes. Add spices; cook, stirring, 2 minutes. Transfer to 4.5-litre slow cooker with chickpeas and the water. Cook, covered, on high, 2½ hours. Season to taste.
3 Serve sprinkled with coriander.

prep + cook time 3 hours
serves 6
nutritional count per serving
22.1g total fat (13.4g saturated fat); 1283kJ (307 cal); 17.9g carbohydrate; 7.2g protein; 6.3g fibre
suitable to freeze at the end of step 2.
serving suggestion Serve with yogurt and rice or naan bread.

AUBERGINE PARMIGIANA

160ml olive oil

1 medium brown onion (150g), chopped finely

2 cloves garlic, crushed

400g canned chopped tomatoes

260g bottled passata

¼ teaspoon dried chilli flakes

2 medium aubergines (600g), sliced thickly

35g plain flour

4 tablespoons fresh basil leaves

200g mozzarella cheese, sliced thinly

50g parmesan cheese, finely grated

½ teaspoon sweet paprika

1 Heat 1 tablespoon of the oil in large frying pan; cook onion, stirring, until onion softens. Add garlic; cook, stirring, until fragrant. Stir in undrained tomatoes, passata and chilli. Transfer to medium jug.

2 Toss aubergine in flour to coat, dust off excess. Heat remaining oil in same pan; cook aubergine, in batches, until browned. Drain on absorbent paper.

3 Layer half the aubergine in 4.5-litre slow cooker; season. Top with half the tomato mixture, basil and mozzarella. Repeat layering, finishing with parmesan. Sprinkle with paprika. Cook, covered, on low, 6 hours.

prep + cook time 6 hours 40 minutes

serves 4

nutritional count per serving
49.9g total fat (12.8g saturated fat); 2562kJ (613 cal); 20.6g carbohydrate; 18.5g protein; 7.2g fibre

not suitable to freeze

serving suggestion Serve with crusty bread and rocket salad or pasta.

ACCOMPANIMENTS: POTATOES

CHEESY MASH

Coarsely chop 1kg potatoes; boil, steam or microwave until tender, drain. Mash potato with 80g finely grated parmesan cheese, 150g finely grated mozzarella cheese, 225g mascarpone cheese and 125ml hot milk in large bowl. Season to taste.

prep + cook time 30 minutes
serves 4
nutritional count per serving
48.1g total fat (31.3g saturated fat); 2763kJ (661 cal); 35.4g carbohydrate; 20.7g protein; 4g fibre

POTATOES ANNA

Preheat oven to 240°C/220°C fan-assisted. Oil shallow 2-litre 26cm round baking dish. Slice 1.2kg potatoes into 2mm slices; pat dry. Melt 100g butter. Place a single layer of potato, slightly overlapping, into dish; brush with a little of the butter. Layer with remaining potato and butter, cover dish with foil; bake 20 minutes. Remove foil; Press down with metal spatula on potato. Reduce oven to 220°C/200°C fan-assisted; bake, uncovered, about 30 minutes or until top is crisp and browned lightly.

prep + cook time 1 hour 15 minutes
serves 6
nutritional count per serving
13.9g total fat (9g saturated fat); 1066kJ (255 cal); 26.3g carbohydrate; 4.9g protein; 3.2g fibre

POTATO CRUSH

Boil, steam or microwave 1kg baby new potatoes until tender; drain. Mash about half the potatoes with 125ml soured cream and 40g softened butter in large bowl until smooth. Using back of a fork or potato masher, gently crush remaining potatoes until skins burst and flesh is just flattened; fold into mash mixture. Season to taste. Sprinkle with 2 tablespoons coarsely chopped flat-leaf parsley.

prep + cook time 20 minutes
serves 4
nutritional count per serving
20.4g total fat (13.2g saturated fat); 1480kJ (354 cal); 33.7g carbohydrate; 6.8g protein; 5g fibre

HASSELBACK POTATOES

Preheat oven to 180°C/160°C fan-assisted. Cut 6 medium potatoes in half horizontally; slice thinly, without cutting all the way through. Coat in combined 40g melted butter and 2 tablespoons olive oil; place in baking dish. Roast, uncovered, 45 minutes, brushing with oil mixture. Roast a further 15 minutes, without brushing, or until potatoes are tender. Sprinkle combined 20g stale breadcrumbs and 60g finely grated cheddar cheese over potatoes; roast about 10 minutes or until browned lightly.

prep + cook time 1 hour 30 minutes
serves 4
nutritional count per serving
22.9g total fat (10g saturated fat); 1756kJ (420 cal); 40.2g carbohydrate; 11.3g protein; 4.7g fibre

ACCOMPANIMENTS: RICE

SPANISH RICE & PEAS

Combine 750ml water and 60ml olive oil in medium saucepan; bring to the boil. Stir in 370g white long-grain rice; cook, uncovered, without stirring, about 10 minutes or until liquid has almost evaporated. Reduce heat; simmer, covered, 5 minutes. Gently stir in 120g frozen peas; simmer, covered, about 5 minutes or until rice and peas are tender. Season to taste.

prep + cook time 30 minutes
serves 6
nutritional count per serving
9.5g total fat (1.4g saturated fat); 1379kJ (330 cal); 54.3g carbohydrate; 5.6g protein; 1.7g fibre

ALMOND PILAF

Melt 20g butter in medium saucepan; cook 1 crushed garlic clove, stirring, until fragrant. Add 185g basmati rice; cook, stirring, 1 minute. Add 250ml chicken stock and 250ml water; bring to the boil. Reduce heat; simmer, covered, about 20 minutes or until rice is tender. Remove from heat; fluff rice with fork. Stir in 3 tablespoons coarsely chopped fresh flat-leaf parsley and 20g roasted flaked almonds. Season to taste.

prep + cook time 35 minutes
serves 4
nutritional count per serving
7.4g total fat (3.1g saturated fat); 1053kJ (252 cal); 40.3g carbohydrate; 5.2g protein; 1.2g fibre

COCONUT RICE

Soak 140g white long-grain rice in cold water 30 minutes. Rinse under cold water until water runs clear; drain. Place 310ml water, 415ml coconut cream, 1 teaspoon granulated sugar, ½ teaspoon ground turmeric, pinch saffron threads and rice in large heavy-based saucepan; cover, bring to the boil, stirring occasionally. Reduce heat; simmer, covered, without stirring, for 15 minutes or until rice is tender. Stand, covered, off the heat, 5 minutes. Season to taste.

prep + cook time 20 minutes
+ standing time
serves 4
nutritional count per serving
21.1g total fat (18.2g saturated fat); 2186kJ (523 cal); 73.9g carbohydrate; 7.7g protein; 2.4g fibre

CLASSIC PULAO

Soak 245g basmati rice in cold water for 20 minutes, drain. Melt 50g butter in large saucepan; stir in 1 finely chopped brown onion and 2 crushed garlic cloves until onion softens. Stir in 1 cinnamon stick and 1 dried bay leaf; cook 2 minutes. Add rice; cook, stirring, 2 minutes. Add 625ml hot chicken stock and 55g sultanas; simmer, covered, about 10 minutes or until rice is tender and liquid is absorbed. Sprinkle with 70g roasted unsalted cashews. Remove cinnamon and season to taste.

prep + cook time 30 minutes + standing time
serves 4
nutritional count per serving
20.6g total fat (8.8g saturated fat); 2128kJ (509 cal); 68.7g carbohydrate; 10.5g protein; 3g fibre

ACCOMPANIMENTS: COUSCOUS & GRAINS

PRESERVED LEMON & MINT COUSCOUS

Combine 200g couscous with 250ml boiling water in medium heatproof bowl, cover; stand about 5 minutes or until water is absorbed, fluffing with fork occasionally. Stir in 1 teaspoon ground cumin, 2 tablespoons finely chopped preserved lemon rind, 80g raisins, 1 large handful coarsely chopped fresh mint and 60ml lemon juice. Season to taste.

prep time 15 minutes
serves 4
nutritional count per serving
0.7g total fat (0.1g saturated fat); 1066kJ (255 cal); 52.8g carbohydrate; 7.4g protein; 2.5g fibre

OLIVE & PARSLEY COUSCOUS

Bring 375ml vegetable stock to the boil in medium saucepan. Remove from heat; stir in 300g couscous and 30g butter. Cover; stand about 5 minutes or until liquid is absorbed, fluffing with fork occasionally. Stir in 180g pitted kalamata olives and 6 tablespoons chopped fresh flat-leaf parsley. Season to taste.

prep + cook time 15 minutes
serves 6
nutritional count per serving
4.9g total fat (2.9g saturated fat); 1074kJ (257 cal); 45.5g carbohydrate; 6.8g protein; 1g fibre

TABBOULEH

Place 40g bulgar wheat in shallow medium bowl. Halve 3 medium tomatoes; scoop pulp from tomato over bulgar. Chop tomato flesh finely; spread over bulgar. Cover; refrigerate 1 hour. Combine bulgar mixture in large bowl with 3 large handfuls coarsely chopped fresh flat-leaf parsley, 3 finely chopped spring onions, 6 tablespoons coarsely chopped fresh mint, 1 crushed garlic clove, 60ml lemon juice and 60ml olive oil. Season to taste.

prep time 30 minutes + refrigeration time

serves 4
nutritional count per serving
14.2g total fat (2g saturated fat); 790kJ (189 cal); 9.4g carbohydrate; 3.6g protein; 5.9g fibre

SPICED LENTILS

Cook 255g red lentils in large saucepan of boiling water until tender; drain. Melt 25g butter in large frying pan; cook 1 finely chopped small brown onion, 1 crushed garlic clove, ½ teaspoon each ground cumin and coriander, ¼ teaspoon each ground turmeric and cayenne pepper, stirring, until onion softens. Add lentils, 125ml chicken stock and 25g butter; cook, stirring, until hot. Remove from heat, stir in 2 tablespoons coarsely chopped fresh flat-leaf parsley. Season to taste.

prep + cook time 20 minutes
serves 4
nutritional count per serving
11.9g total fat (7g saturated fat); 1354kJ (324 cal); 29.9g carbohydrate; 18.9g protein; 10.8g fibre

ACCOMPANIMENTS: VEGETABLES

CREAMED SPINACH

Melt 20g butter in large frying pan; cook 600g spinach, stirring, until wilted. Add 125ml single cream; bring to the boil. Reduce heat; simmer, uncovered, until liquid reduces by half. Blend or process mixture until smooth; season to taste.

prep + cook time 15 minutes
serves 4
nutritional count per serving
38.7g total fat (25.4g saturated fat); 1555kJ (372 cal); 2.8g carbohydrate; 3.5g protein; 2.1g fibre

ROASTED CARAMELISED PARSNIPS

Preheat oven to 220°C/200°C fan-assisted. Halve 1kg parsnips lengthways. Combine parsnips with 2 tablespoons olive oil, 55g light brown sugar and 1 teaspoon ground nutmeg in large baking dish, season; roast about 1 hour or until parsnips are browned and tender. Serve parsnips sprinkled with 1 tablespoon finely chopped fresh flat-leaf parsley.

prep + cook time 1 hour 10 minutes
serves 4
nutritional count per serving
9.6g total fat (1.3g saturated fat); 1074kJ (257 cal); 35.8g carbohydrate; 4.1g protein; 5.7g fibre

FRESH PEAS, CARAWAY & PARMESAN

Melt 60g butter in large frying pan; cook 1 teaspoon caraway seeds, 2 teaspoons finely grated lemon rind and 1 thinly sliced small red onion, stirring, until onion softens. Add 480g shelled fresh peas; cook, stirring, until peas are just tender. Stir in 4 tablespoons coarsely chopped fresh flat-leaf parsley then sprinkle with 40g finely grated parmesan cheese.

prep + cook time 40 minutes
serves 6
nutritional count per serving
8.1g total fat (5.1g saturated fat); 598kJ (143 cal); 8.5g carbohydrate; 6.8g protein; 4.8g fibre
tip You need about 1.3kg fresh pea pods to get the amount of peas required for this recipe.

TOMATO-BRAISED BEANS

Heat 1 tablespoon olive oil in large saucepan; cook 1 coarsely chopped medium brown onion and 2 crushed garlic cloves, stirring, until onion softens. Add 1kg trimmed green beans and 4 coarsely chopped medium tomatoes; cook, covered, stirring occasionally, about 20 minutes or until vegetables soften slightly. Season to taste.

prep + cook time 35 minutes
serves 6
nutritional count per serving
3.5g total fat (0.4g saturated fat); 397kJ (95 cal); 7.4g carbohydrate; 6.2g fibre

DESSERTS

PASSIONFRUIT CRÈME CARAMELS

110g caster sugar
60ml water
2 tablespoons passionfruit pulp
250ml milk
180ml single cream
2 x 5cm pieces lemon rind
3 eggs
2 egg yolks
75g caster sugar, extra

1 Stir sugar and the water in small saucepan over high heat, without boiling, until sugar dissolves; bring to the boil. Boil, uncovered, without stirring, until mixture is deep caramel in colour. Remove from heat; allow bubbles to subside, gently stir in passionfruit pulp. Divide toffee mixture into six greased 125ml metal moulds. Place moulds in 4.5-litre slow cooker.

2 Meanwhile, combine milk, cream and rind in medium saucepan; bring to the boil. Whisk eggs, egg yolks and extra sugar in large bowl until combined; gradually whisk in hot milk mixture. Strain mixture into large jug; discard rind. Pour mixture into moulds. Pour enough boiling water into cooker to come halfway up sides of moulds.

3 Cook, covered, on low, about 1½ hours or until crème caramels feel firm. Remove moulds from cooker. Cover moulds; refrigerate overnight.

4 Gently ease crème caramels from sides of moulds; invert onto serving plates.

prep + cook time 2 hours 20 minutes + refrigeration time
makes 6
nutritional count per serving
19.1g total fat (11.1g saturated fat); 1371kJ (328 cal); 34.2g carbohydrate; 6.6g protein; 0.9g fibre
not suitable to freeze

SOURED CREAM CHEESECAKE

500g cream cheese, softened
150g caster sugar
1 teaspoon vanilla extract
2 eggs
120g soured cream
60ml lemon juice
1 tablespoon plain flour
125g digestive biscuits
80g butter, melted

1 Grease 2-litre pudding basin. Cut two long strips of baking parchment; place strips on inside of basin, crossing over at the bottom, extending 5cm over side of steamer (see tip).

2 Beat cream cheese, sugar and vanilla in small bowl with electric mixer until smooth. Add eggs, soured cream, juice and flour; beat until smooth. Spoon mixture into basin.

3 Place basin in 4.5-litre slow cooker; pour enough boiling water into cooker to come halfway up side of basin. Cook, covered, on low, 1 hour.

4 Meanwhile, blend or process biscuits until fine. Add butter; process until combined. Remove lid from cooker. Press biscuit mixture on top of cheesecake; top with three layers of absorbent paper. Cook, covered, on low, for a further 45 minutes.

5 Remove basin from cooker; cool. Cover; refrigerate overnight.

prep + cook time 2 hours 15 minutes + cooling & refrigeration time
serves 8
nutritional count per serving 38.7g total fat (24.2g saturated fat); 2119kJ (507 cal); 33.2g carbohydrate; 8.6g protein; 0.4g fibre
not suitable to freeze
serving suggestion Serve with double cream, some sliced strawberries and drizzled with passionfruit pulp.
tip The baking parchment strips are used to help remove the cheesecake from the basin once it's been refrigerated overnight. Place the basin upside down on a serving plate, gently pull on the paper strips and the cheesecake will ease away from the side of the basin.

RHUBARB & ORANGE COMPOTE

16 large trimmed stems rhubarb
  (1kg), chopped coarsely
1 teaspoon finely grated orange
  rind
2 large oranges (600g), peeled,
  sliced thickly
150g unrefined caster sugar
60ml cranberry juice
1 teaspoon each ground ginger
  and cinnamon
80g flaked almonds, roasted

cinnamon yogurt cream
125ml double cream
140g greek-style yogurt
½ teaspoon cinnamon sugar

1 Grease 4.5-litre slow cooker
bowl.
2 Combine rhubarb, rind, orange,
sugar, juice and spices in cooker.
Cook, covered, on low, about
3½ hours or until rhubarb is
tender. Remove bowl from cooker.
Stand 20 minutes before serving.
3 Meanwhile, make cinnamon
yogurt cream.
4 Divide rhubarb mixture into
serving bowls; top with cinnamon
yogurt cream and nuts.

cinnamon yogurt cream
Combine ingredients in small
bowl.

prep + cook time 4 hours
+ standing time
serves 6
nutritional count per serving
20.5g total fat (8.8g saturated
fat); 1580kJ (378 cal); 37.7g
carbohydrate; 7.7g protein;
6.3g fibre
not suitable to freeze

CROISSANT CUSTARD PUDDING WITH STRAWBERRIES

4 croissants (200g)
160g strawberry jam
80g white eating chocolate, chopped finely
625ml milk
600ml single cream
110g caster sugar
1 teaspoon vanilla extract
6 eggs

macerated strawberries
250g strawberries, halved
1 tablespoon orange-flavoured liqueur
1 tablespoon icing sugar

1 Grease 4.5-litre slow cooker bowl.
2 Split croissants in half; spread cut-sides with jam; sprinkle chocolate over half the croissants, sandwich with remaining croissants. Place croissants in slow cooker.
3 Combine milk, cream, sugar and extract in medium saucepan; bring to the boil. Whisk eggs in large bowl; gradually whisk in hot milk mixture. Pour custard over croissants; stand 10 minutes.
4 Cook, covered, on low, about 2 hours 45 minutes, or until firm (do not lift the lid during the cooking process, see tip).
5 Meanwhile, make macerated strawberries.
6 Remove bowl from cooker. Stand pudding 5 minutes before serving. Serve pudding with macerated strawberries and drizzled with a little extra cream.

macerated strawberries
Combine ingredients in medium bowl; stand 30 minutes.

prep + cook time 3 hours 15 minutes + standing time
serves 8
nutritional count per serving 44.7g total fat (28.8g saturated fat); 2658kJ (636 cal); 51.4g carbohydrate; 7.9g protein; 1.7g fibre
not suitable to freeze
serving suggestion Serve pudding with ice-cream and/or cream.
tip It's important not to lift the lid during the cooking of the pudding, as the condensation runs down the side of the cooker and causes damp patches on the pudding.

STICKY DATE & FIG STEAMED PUDDING

300g pitted dried dates, finely
   chopped
100g dried figs, finely chopped
250ml water
220g light brown sugar
90g butter, chopped coarsely
1 teaspoon bicarbonate of soda
2 eggs, beaten lightly
110g plain flour
110g self-raising flour

butterscotch sauce
165g light brown sugar
250ml single cream
125g unsalted butter, chopped
   coarsely

1 Combine fruit, the water, sugar and butter in medium saucepan; stir over heat until butter melts and sugar dissolves. Bring to the boil. Reduce heat; simmer, uncovered, 5 minutes. Transfer mixture to large heatproof bowl, stir in soda; cool 10 minutes.
2 Stir eggs and sifted dry ingredients into fruit mixture.
3 Grease 2-litre pudding basin; spoon mixture into basin. Top with pleated baking parchment and foil; secure with kitchen string.
4 Place basin in 4.5-litre slow cooker; pour enough boiling water into cooker to come halfway up side of basin. Cook, covered, on high, 5 hours, replenishing with boiling water as necessary to maintain level.
5 Remove pudding from cooker. Stand 10 minutes before turning onto plate.
6 Meanwhile, make butterscotch sauce.
7 Serve pudding drizzled with butterscotch sauce.

butterscotch sauce Stir ingredients in medium saucepan over heat, without boiling, until sugar dissolves; bring to the boil. Reduce heat; simmer, uncovered, 2 minutes.

prep + cook time 5 hours 30 minutes + standing time
serves 12
nutritional count per serving
24.9g total fat (15.9g saturated fat); 2174kJ (520 cal); 70.6g carbohydrate; 4.4g protein; 4.3g fibre
suitable to freeze at the end of step 5
serving suggestion Serve with thick cream or ice-cream.

GLOSSARY

bamboo shoots tender shoots of bamboo plants, available in cans; drain and rinse before use.

bicarbonate of soda also called baking soda; a leavening agent.

bulgur wheat also known as burghul; hulled steamed wheat kernels that, once dried, are crushed into various size grains.

cajun seasoning packaged mix of herbs and spices; can include paprika, basil, onion, fennel, thyme, cayenne and white pepper.

caraway seeds a member of the parsley family; available in seed or ground form.

cavolo nero also known as tuscan cabbage; a staple in Tuscan country cooking. It has long, narrow, wrinkled leaves and a rich and astringent, mild cabbage flavour. It doesn't lose its volume like spinach when cooked, but it does need longer cooking.

cheese

cheddar the most common cow's milk cheese; should be aged and hard.

cream a soft cow's-milk cheese with a fat content ranging from 14 per cent to 33 per cent.

mascarpone a cultured cream product made in much the same way as yogurt. Whitish to creamy yellow in colour, it has a soft, creamy texture.

mozzarella a semi-soft cheese with a delicate, fresh taste; has a low melting point and stringy texture when hot.

parmesan a sharp-tasting, dry, hard cheese, made from skimmed or semi-skimmed milk and aged for at least a year.

ricotta a soft, sweet, moist, white, cow's-milk cheese with a low fat content (about 8.5 per cent) and a slightly grainy texture. The name roughly translates as 'cooked again' and refers to ricotta's manufacture from a whey that is itself a by-product of other cheese making.

chillies available in many types and sizes, both fresh and dried. The smaller the chilli, the hotter it is. Wear rubber gloves when handling chillies, as they can burn your skin. Removing seeds and membranes lessens the heat level.

chilli flakes deep-red in colour; dehydrated, extremely fine slices and whole seeds; good for cooking or for sprinkling over cooked food.

chilli powder the Asian variety is the hottest, made from ground chillies; it can be used as a substitute for fresh chillies in the proportion of ½ teaspoon ground chilli powder to 1 medium chopped fresh chilli.

chorizo a sausage of Spanish origin; made of coarsely ground pork and seasoned with garlic and chillies.

coconut cream available in tins and cartons; the proportions are usually two parts coconut to one part water.

coconut milk unsweetened coconut milk available in cans.

cornflour also known as cornstarch; used as a thickening agent in cooking.

couscous a fine, grain-like cereal product, made from semolina.

fish sauce also called nam pla or nuoc nam; made from pulverised salted fermented fish, mostly anchovies. Has a pungent smell and strong taste; use sparingly.

garam masala a blend of spices based on varying proportions of cardamom, cinnamon, cloves, coriander, fennel and cumin, roasted and ground together. Black pepper and chilli can be added for a hotter version.

ghee clarified butter; with the milk solids removed, this fat can be heated to a very high temperature without burning.

harissa a North African paste made from dried red chillies, garlic, olive oil and caraway seeds; can be used as a rub for meat, an ingredient in sauces and dressings, or eaten on its own as a condiment. It is available, ready-made, in most supermarkets.

kaffir lime leaves aromatic leaves used fresh or dried in Asian dishes. A strip of fresh lime peel may be substituted for each kaffir lime leaf.

moroccan seasoning available from most Middle-Eastern food stores, spice shops and major supermarkets. A blend of turmeric, cinnamon and cumin; use ras el hanout if unavailable.

mushrooms

button small, cultivated white mushrooms with a delicate, subtle flavour.

chestnut light to dark brown mushrooms with mild, earthy flavour.

porcini firm, nutty-flavoured Italian mushroom. Dried porcini mushrooms are widely available and add a strong flavour to pasta, soups and sauces.

mustard

dijon a pale brown, distinctively flavoured fairly mild French mustard.

wholegrain also known as seeded; a French-style coarse-grain mustard made from crushed mustard seeds and Dijon-style French mustard.

okra also known as gumbo or lady's fingers; a green, ridged, oblong pod with a furry skin. Used in Caribbean, Indian, Mediterranean, Middle-Eastern and southern-American cooking, it is used to thicken stews. Rinse and cut off capped end close to stalk.

onions

brown their pungent flesh adds flavour to a vast range of dishes.

red also known as spanish, red spanish or bermuda onion; a sweet-flavoured, large, purple-red onion.

pickling also known as cocktail onions, these baby brown onions are larger than shallots. To peel, cover with boiling water and stand for 2 minutes, then drain. The skins will slip off easily.

shallots also called eschalots; small, elongated, brown-skinned members of the onion family. They grow in tight clusters similar to garlic.

palm sugar also called nam tan pip, jaggery, jawa or gula melaka; made from the sap of the sugar palm tree. Light brown to black in colour; usually sold in rock-hard cakes. If unavailable, use brown sugar.

paprika ground dried red pepper; available sweet, smoked or hot.

passata thick sauce made from ripe tomatoes that have been puréed and sieved to remove the skin and seeds.

preserved lemon a North African specialty, the citrus is preserved, usually whole, in a mixture of salt and lemon juice or oil. To use, remove and discard pulp, squeeze juice from rind, then rinse rind well before slicing thinly. Available from specialty food shops, delicatessens and good supermarkets.

rice

arborio small, round-grain rice; especially suitable for risottos.

basmati fragrant, long-grained white rice. Wash several times before cooking.

jasmine sometimes sold as Thai fragrant rice, Jasmine rice is so-named due to its sweet aroma. Available from most supermarkets.

long grain elongated grain, remains separate when cooked; most popular steaming rice in Asia.

rigani Greek oregano with a sweet, spicy aroma. If unavailable, you can substitute marjoram.

rosewater extract made from crushed rose petals; available from health food stores and good supermarkets.

soy sauce highly flavoured, salty sauce made from fermented soya beans. Several variations are available in most supermarkets. We use a mild Japanese variety in our recipes; possibly the best table soy and the one to choose if you only want one variety.

star anise a dried star-shaped pod, the seeds of which taste of aniseed.

thai basil sweet, aromatic basil native to Southeast Asia. You can substitute the more common variety, but the taste will not be the same.

vanilla

bean dried long, thin pod from a tropical golden orchid grown in central and South America and Tahiti; the minuscule black seeds inside the bean are used to impart a distinctively sweet vanilla flavour.

extract obtained from vanilla beans infused in water; a non-alcoholic version of essence.

vinegar

cider made from fermented apples.

sherry mellow wine vinegar named for its colour.

white made from spirit of cane sugar.

white wine based on fermented white wine.

INDEX